New York
LIBERTY

by Charlie Beattie

Copyright © 2026 by Press Room Editions. All rights reserved. No part of this book may be used or reproduced in any manner whatsoever, including internet usage, without written permission from the copyright owner, except in the case of brief quotations embodied in critical articles and reviews.

Book design by Kate Liestman
Cover design by Kate Liestman

Photographs ©: Abbie Parr/AP Images, cover; David Berding/Getty Images Sport/Getty Images, 4, 7, 9; Todd Warshaw/Allsport/Getty Images Sport/Getty Images, 10; Craig Jones/Allsport/Getty Images Sport/Getty Images, 13; Brett Coomer/AP Images, 15; Chad Rachman/AP Images, 16; Tim Clayton/Corbis Sport/Getty Images, 19; Leon Bennett/Getty Images Sport/Getty Images, 21; Steph Chambers/Getty Images Sport/Getty Images, 22; Mitchell Leff/Getty Images Sport/Getty Images, 25; Elsa/Getty Images Sport/Getty Images, 27; Sarah Stier/Getty Images Sport/Getty Images, 29

Press Box Books, an imprint of Press Room Editions.

ISBN
979-8-89469-017-9 (library bound)
979-8-89469-030-8 (paperback)
979-8-89469-055-1 (epub)
979-8-89469-043-8 (hosted ebook)

Library of Congress Control Number: 2025931640

Distributed by North Star Editions, Inc.
2297 Waters Drive
Mendota Heights, MN 55120
www.northstareditions.com

Printed in the United States of America
082025

ABOUT THE AUTHOR

Charlie Beattie is a writer, editor, and former sportscaster. Originally from Saint Paul, Minnesota, he now lives in Charleston, South Carolina, with his wife and son.

TABLE OF CONTENTS

CHAPTER 1
DEEP SHOT   5

CHAPTER 2
RUNNERS UP   11

CHAPTER 3
BIG NAMES   17

CHAPTER 4
CHAMPIONS AT LAST   23

SUPERSTAR PROFILE
BREANNA STEWART   28

QUICK STATS   30
GLOSSARY   31
TO LEARN MORE   32
INDEX   32

CHAPTER 1

DEEP SHOT

New York Liberty guard Sabrina Ionescu knew her moment was coming. Game 3 of the 2024 Women's National Basketball Association (WNBA) Finals was tied 77–77 with just seconds to play. The series was also tied, 1–1. More than 19,000 Minnesota Lynx fans were hoping for

Sabrina Ionescu averaged 16.9 points per game in the 2024 playoffs.

a stop. Ionescu wanted to send them all home unhappy.

Game 3 had been an uphill battle for New York. The Lynx had led by 10 after the first quarter. And they led by eight at halftime. But the Liberty were loaded with star players. They stepped up when the team needed them most.

Forward Breanna Stewart had led New York's comeback. She scored 30 points. She also grabbed 11 rebounds and blocked four shots. Center Jonquel Jones added 13 points. Ionescu had been quiet, though. Going into the game's final seconds, she'd scored only 10 points. But New York coach Sandy Brondello had confidence in her team's best shooter.

Breanna Stewart (30) led the Liberty in scoring during the 2024 Finals.

With the game on the line, Brondello drew up a play for Ionescu.

Ionescu set up on the left sideline. She passed the ball inbounds. Teammate Leonie Fiebich received the pass. Then she handed it right back to Ionescu.

The seconds ticked down. Ionescu stood on the Lynx logo at center court. She dribbled slowly back and forth as she stared down Minnesota guard Kayla McBride.

With four seconds to go, Ionescu made her move. She jabbed to her right. McBride fell for the fake. Ionescu then darted back to her left. She stood 28 feet (9 m) from the basket when she pulled up for her shot. The three-pointer was

A YEAR TO REMEMBER

The WNBA's 2024 regular season was the most-watched season in league history. The same was true for the 2024 Finals. More than 1 million fans tuned in to each game. Game 5 drew 3.3 million viewers. It was the most-watched WNBA game in 25 years.

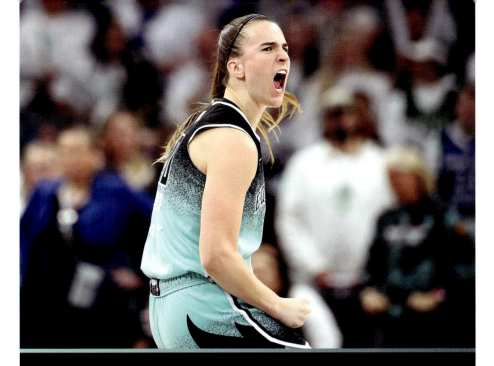

Ionescu celebrates her game-winning shot in Game 3 of the 2024 Finals.

right on target. The Minnesota crowd fell silent as the ball went through the basket.

The Lynx still had one second left to tie the game. But McBride's desperation shot didn't come close. Thanks to Ionescu, the Liberty now held a 2–1 series lead. Her clutch shooting had given New York a huge advantage in the series.

CHAPTER 2

RUNNERS UP

On October 30, 1996, the New York Liberty became one of the WNBA's first eight teams. The team announced its nickname that day. Soon, the Liberty added two great players. Forward Rebecca Lobo and guard Teresa Weatherspoon had been big stars in college. Now they were ready to help the new league grow.

Rebecca Lobo shoots during the first-ever WNBA game.

New York traveled to face the Los Angeles Sparks on June 21, 1997. The teams played in the first game in league history. Lobo led the way with 16 points. Weatherspoon added 10 assists. New York won 67–57. The Liberty finished 17–11 in their first season. They made a run to the championship game. But the Houston Comets won 65–51.

Knee injuries slowed down Lobo's career. However, Weatherspoon remained one of New York's most exciting players for years. "T-Spoon" didn't score a lot. But she was one of the league's best passers and defenders. She also showed great leadership. Weatherspoon always pushed her teammates to play better.

Teresa Weatherspoon won the Defensive Player of the Year Award in 1997 and 1998.

The Liberty reached the Finals again in 1999 and 2000. Both times, they lost to Houston. In 2002, Weatherspoon became the first WNBA player to record both 1,000 points and 1,000 assists in a career. She also led her team back to the Finals that season. Unfortunately for Liberty fans, New York lost again. This time, the Liberty fell to the Sparks.

Witherspoon left the team after the

THE SHOT

In Game 2 of the 1999 WNBA Finals, the Liberty trailed the Houston Comets 67-65 with two seconds left. Teresa Weatherspoon took the inbounds pass. She didn't have time to go the full length of the court. So, she rose up at half-court and lobbed a one-handed shot. The ball banked in. New York won 68-67. More than two decades later, "The Shot" is still one of the WNBA's most famous plays.

Liberty players celebrate after Weatherspoon's game-winning shot in Game 2 of the 1999 Finals.

2003 season. Without their leader, the Liberty struggled to get back to the Finals. But a new set of stars were about to step up in the Big Apple.

CHAPTER 3

BIG NAMES

The Liberty already had a worthy replacement for Teresa Weatherspoon. Becky Hammon had been Weatherspoon's backup at point guard since 1999. Hammon made the All-Star Game for the first time in 2003. Liberty fans loved the way Hammon played. The rugged guard went all out on both ends of the court.

Becky Hammon played in the All-Star Game three times with the Liberty.

She led New York in scoring each season from 2004 to 2006.

The Liberty traded away Hammon before the 2007 season. After that, it took New York a few seasons to find another star. The team traded for guard Cappie Pondexter in 2010. Pondexter was lightning quick. She led New York to a team-record 22 wins.

New York faced the Indiana Fever in the opening round of the 2010 playoffs. The score was tied 74–74 late in a decisive Game 3. Pondexter hit a layup as she fell out of bounds. The basket put New York up for good. The Liberty won 77–74. In the semifinals, Pondexter tallied 60 points over two games. But her scoring wasn't

In 2010, Cappie Pondexter (23) averaged a career-high 21.4 points per game.

enough. The Atlanta Dream swept the Liberty.

New York traded Pondexter before the 2015 season. The Liberty picked up creative guard Epiphanny Prince to replace her. Prince teamed up with dominant center Tina Charles. The duo led the Liberty to 23 wins that year. New York reached the semifinals again. In Game 1 against the Fever, Charles nearly had a triple-double. She finished with 18 points, 7 rebounds, and 9 assists. New York won 84–67. However, the Liberty lost the next two games. Once again, they came up just short of the Finals.

Charles remained one of the WNBA's best players through the 2019 season. But the Liberty had

> ## NEW OWNER, NEW HOME
>
> The Liberty had played in several arenas since their first season. In 2019, Joe Tsai bought the team. He also owned the Brooklyn Nets of the National Basketball Association (NBA). Tsai moved the Liberty into the Nets' arena in Brooklyn, New York.

Tina Charles (31) averaged 18.7 points per game during her six seasons with the Liberty.

slipped in the standings. After Charles left, the team won only two games in the 2020 season. Even so, it wouldn't be long before the Liberty were contenders again.

CHAPTER 4

CHAMPIONS AT LAST

In 2020, the Liberty selected Sabrina Ionescu with the top pick in the draft. Fans expected the point guard to be New York's next big star. However, an ankle injury ended her rookie season after just three games. She returned healthy in 2021, though. And she led her team back to the playoffs.

Through 2024, Ionescu had averaged at least four assists per game in every season of her career.

Before the 2023 season, New York gave the sharpshooting Ionescu plenty of help. The team traded for Jonquel Jones. The center could score from inside and outside the three-point arc. And she grabbed plenty of rebounds. New York's biggest addition was Breanna Stewart. The versatile forward had won two WNBA titles with the Seattle Storm.

The trio led New York to a 32–8 record. But the Liberty fell short in the Finals against the Las Vegas Aces. The team bounced back in 2024. Once again, the Liberty won 32 games in the regular season.

The Liberty reached the Finals again. This time, they faced the Minnesota Lynx.

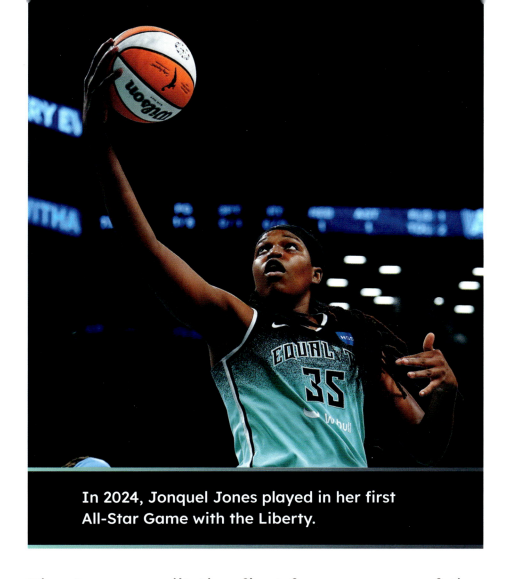

In 2024, Jonquel Jones played in her first All-Star Game with the Liberty.

The teams split the first four games of the series. New York hosted Game 5, which would decide the champion. In the fourth quarter, the Liberty trailed. But they rallied to tie the game and force overtime.

REVERSING FORTUNES

The Commissioner's Cup is an in-season tournament that the WNBA started in 2021. In 2023, the Liberty won the tournament for the first time. They defeated the Las Vegas Aces 82–63. However, Las Vegas beat New York in that year's WNBA Finals. A year later, New York lost to the Minnesota Lynx in the Commissioner's Cup final. But New York went on to beat Minnesota in the Finals.

Stewart and Ionescu struggled to score for most of the game. In overtime, other players stepped up. Leonie Fiebich took a quick pass and hit a three-pointer from the wing. The shot gave New York a 63–60 lead just seconds into the extra period. Backup center Nyara Sabally then made a key steal. She raced down for a layup. Later, Sabally blocked a

The Liberty celebrate after winning the 2024 Finals.

Minnesota shot. The Liberty held the Lynx to just two points in overtime. New York won 67–62. After years of heartbreaking losses, the Liberty were finally champions!

SUPERSTAR PROFILE

BREANNA STEWART

Breanna Stewart became a free agent after the 2022 season. Every WNBA team wanted her. She chose to play for the Liberty. Stewart had already won the league's Most Valuable Player (MVP) Award in 2018. She was one of the biggest stars in the WNBA. Now she wanted to play in the league's largest city to help the WNBA grow.

Stewart did just that. She also helped the Liberty become a contender. The versatile forward lifted New York from 16 wins in 2022 to 32 in 2023. That year, Stewart earned MVP honors for the second time.

The next season, Stewart did it all for New York. She led the team in points, blocks, and steals per game. She also hit two key free throws in the final seconds of Game 5 of the Finals. The shots forced overtime. The Liberty could always count on Stewart to step up when they needed her.

In 2024, Stewart made the All-WNBA First Team for the sixth time.

QUICK STATS

NEW YORK LIBERTY

Founded: 1997

Championships: 1 (2024)

Key coaches:
- Richie Adubato (1999-2004): 100-78, 14-13 playoffs
- Bill Laimbeer (2013-17): 92-78, 3-5 playoffs
- Sandy Brondello (2022-): 80-36, 15-9 playoffs, 1 WNBA title

Most career points: Tina Charles (3,739)

Most career assists: Teresa Weatherspoon (1,306)

Most career rebounds: Tina Charles (1,723)

Most career blocks: Kiah Stokes (195)

Most career steals: Teresa Weatherspoon (453)

Stats are accurate through the 2024 season.

GLOSSARY

assists
Passes that lead directly to a teammate scoring a basket.

clutch
Having to do with a difficult situation when the outcome of the game is in question.

contenders
Teams that are good enough to win a title.

draft
An event that allows teams to choose new players coming into the league.

free agent
A player who can sign with any team.

overtime
An additional period of play to decide a game's winner.

swept
Won all the games in a series.

triple-double
When a player reaches 10 or more of three different statistics in one game.

versatile
Able to perform many tasks well.

TO LEARN MORE

Graves, Will. *Basketball*. Abdo Publishing, 2024.
O'Neal, Ciara. *The WNBA Finals*. Apex Editions, 2023.
Whiting, Jim, *The Story of the New York Liberty*.
   Creative Education, 2024.

MORE INFORMATION

To learn more about the New York Liberty, go to **pressboxbooks.com/AllAccess**. These links are routinely monitored and updated to provide the most current information available.

INDEX

Atlanta Dream, 19

Brondello, Sandy, 6–7

Charles, Tina, 20–21

Fiebich, Leonie, 7, 26

Hammon, Becky, 17–18
Houston Comets, 12, 14

Indiana Fever, 18, 20
Ionescu, Sabrina, 5–9, 23–24, 26

Jones, Jonquel, 6, 24

Las Vegas Aces, 24, 26
Lobo, Rebecca, 11–12
Los Angeles Sparks, 12, 14

McBride, Kayla, 8–9
Minnesota Lynx, 5–6, 8–9, 24–27

Pondexter, Cappie, 18–19
Prince, Epiphanny, 19

Sabally, Nyara, 26–27
Seattle Storm, 24
Stewart, Breanna, 6, 24, 26, 28

Tsai, Joe, 20

Weatherspoon, Teresa, 11–12, 14–15, 17